Dear Maria,

I'm so happy and grateful
that you are willing answer language
for me....

Happy Birthday

P.S. next year Birthday's notes
will be in arabic or French.

Lili

10. Nov. 2018

The Arabic Alphabet

Remember it Letter by Letter

Written by Sam Burr
Designed & Illustrated by Jocelyn Affleck

alif

alif is for a'laa - It is the highest letter!

a'laa - Highest - أَعْلَى

baa

baa is for buqa'a - It has just one spot!

buqa'a - Spot - بُقَعَةٌ

taa

taa is for tawaa'im - It has two dots like twins!

tawaa'im - Twins - تَوَائِمُ

thaa

thaa is for thalaatha - It has three dots on top!

thalaatha - Three - ثَلَاثَةٌ

jeem

jeem is for jumjumah - A skull with a eye inside!

jumjumah - Skull - جُمْجُمَةٌ

Haa

Haa is for Hufrah - It is empty like hole!

Hufra - Hole - حُفْرَةٌ

khaa

khaa is for khaarij - Its dot is outside!

khaarij - Outside - خَارِجٌ

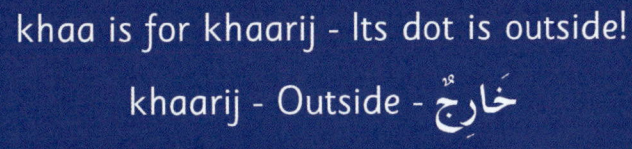

ﺩ

daal

daal is for duudah - It curls like a worm!

duudah - Worm - دُوْدَةٌ

dhaal

dhaal is for dhubaaba - It sounds like a fly!

dhubaaba - Fly - ذُبَابَةٌ

raa

raa is for rub' - It is a quarter of a circle!

rubu' - Quarter - رُبْعْ

zay

zay is for zalzaal - It sounds like an earthquake!

zalzaal - Earthquake - زَلْزَالٌ

seen

seen is for sinn - It has three teeth!

sinn - Tooth - سِنّ

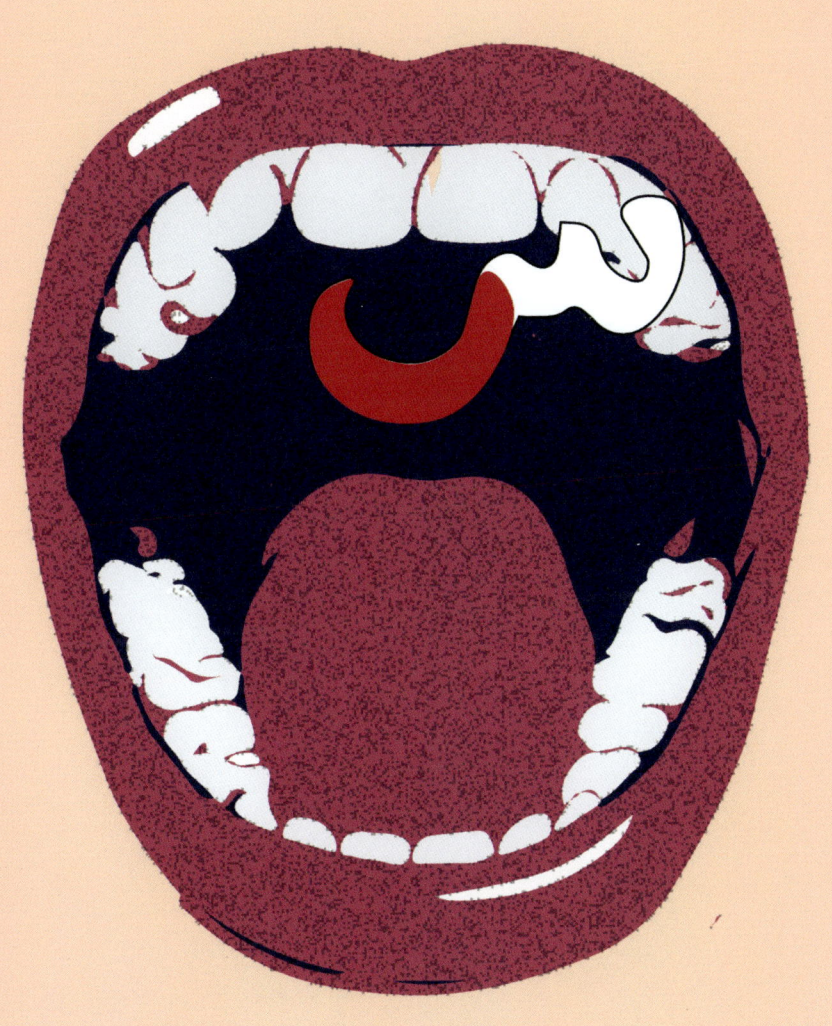

sheen

sheen is for shakhshakha - It sprays out three dots!

shakhshakha - Spray - شَخْشَخ

Saad

Saad is for Sawt - Say it with a deep voice!
Sawt - Voice - صَوْتٌ

Daad

Daad is for Darb because it sounds like hitting a drum:
Dad-Dad-Dad!

Darb - Hit - ضَرْبٌ

Taa

Taa is for Taweel - It is such a tall letter!

Taweel - Tall - طَوِيْلٌ

DHhaa

DHa is for DHann - I think it's hard to say!

DHann - Think - ظَنّ

Ayn

'Ayn is for 'unuq - Pronounce it from your neck!

'unuq - Neck - عُنقٌ

ghain

ghain is for ghumghuma - It sounds like a grumble!

ghumghuma - Grumble - غَمْغَمَ

faa

faa is for feel - It has a long trunk like an elephant!

feel - Elephant - فِيْلٌ

qaaf

qaaf is for qamar - It is round like the moon!

qamar - Moon - قَمَرٌ

kaaf

kaaf as in rukn - It has sharp corners!

rukn - Corner - رُكْنٌ

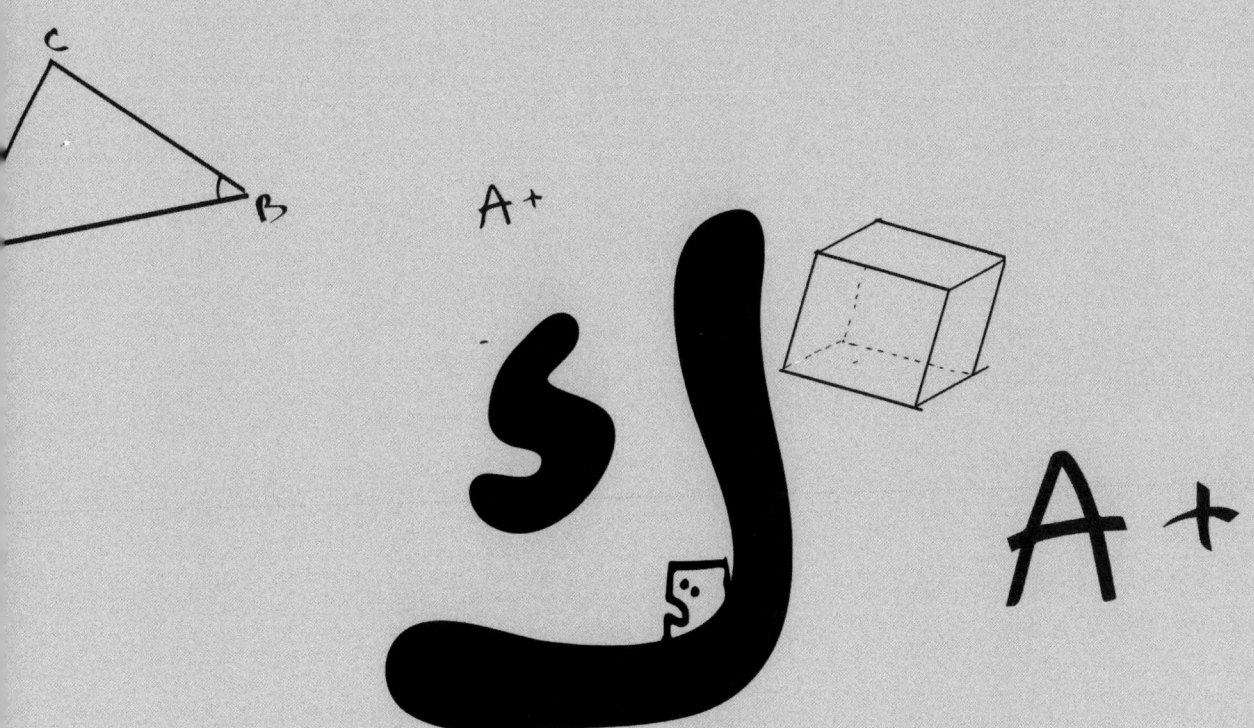

laam

laam as in lahdham - It is sharp and pointed!

lahdham - Sharp - لَهذَمٌ

miim

miim as in humhuma - It sounds like a hum!

humhuma - Hum - هَمْهَم

nuun

nuun as in nuqTah - It has one dot on top!

nuqTah - Dot - نُقْطَة

haa

haa is for hawaa' - It sounds like a breath of air!

hawaa' - Air - هَوَاءٌ

waw

waw is for waswaas - It sounds like a whisperer!

waswaas - Whisperer - وَسْوَاسٌ

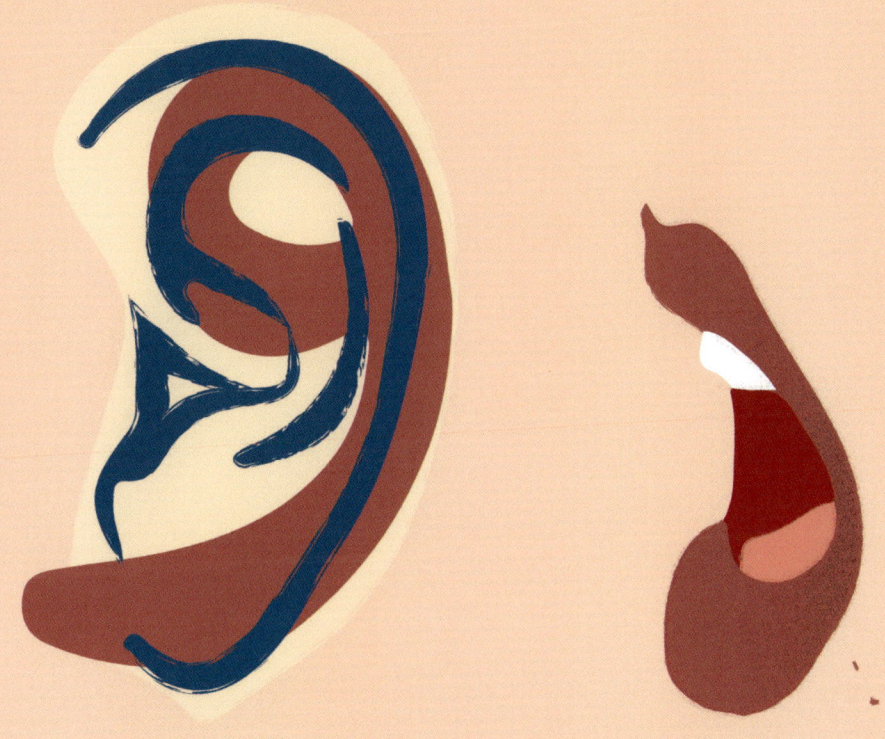

yaa

yaa is for yanhani - because its shape bends!

yanhani - It bends - يَنْحَنِي

Printed in Great Britain
by Amazon